Buddy BOOKS
Prehistoric Animals

Giant Armadillo

ABDO
Publishing Company

A Buddy Book
by
Michael P. Goecke

VISIT US AT
www.abdopub.com

Published by Buddy Books, an imprint of ABDO Publishing Company, 4940 Viking Drive, Edina, Minnesota 55435. Copyright © 2004 by Abdo Consulting Group, Inc. International copyrights reserved in all countries. No part of this book may be reproduced in any form without written permission from the publisher.

Printed in the United States.

Edited by: Christy DeVillier
Contributing Editor: Matt Ray
Graphic Design: Deborah Coldiron
Image Research: Deborah Coldiron
Illustrations: Deborah Coldiron, Denise Esner, Maria Hosley
Photographs: Eyewire, Hulton Archives, Steve McHugh, Photodisc

Library of Congress Cataloging-in-Publication Data

Goecke, Michael P., 1968-
    Giant armadillo / Michael P. Goecke.
        p. cm. — (Prehistoric animals. Set II)
    Summary: Introduces the physical characteristics, habitat, and behavior of this prehistoric relative of modern-day armadillos.
    Includes bibliographical references and index.
ISBN 1-57765-974-0
    1. Glyptodon—Juvenile literature. [1. Glyptodon. 2. Mammals, Fossil. 3. Prehistoric animals. 4. Paleontology.] I. Title.

QE882.E2 G62 2003
569'.31—dc21
                                                2002032277

Table of Contents

Animals that lived more than 5,500 years ago are called prehistoric. The dinosaurs were prehistoric animals. They roamed the world millions of years ago. This time is often called the Age of Dinosaurs.

Many exciting prehistoric animals lived after the dinosaurs. Some of these animals were mammals. The Age of Mammals has lasted for millions of years. Some prehistoric mammals were saber-toothed cats, woolly mammoths, and giant armadillos.

Prehistoric Animals

5

The Giant Armadillo

Glyptodon

(GLIP-toh-don)

The *Glyptodon* was a prehistoric armadillo. It was bigger than today's armadillos. So some people call the *Glyptodon* "giant armadillo."

There are 20 kinds of armadillos around today. They live in warm parts of North America and South America. Today's armadillos are related to anteaters and sloths. They are also related to the prehistoric giant armadillo.

This armadillo is related to the prehistoric *Glyptodon*.

The giant armadillo was as big as a small car. It grew to become about five feet (two m) tall. Adults were about 12 feet (4 m) long. Some weighed as much as 4,000 pounds (1,814 kg).

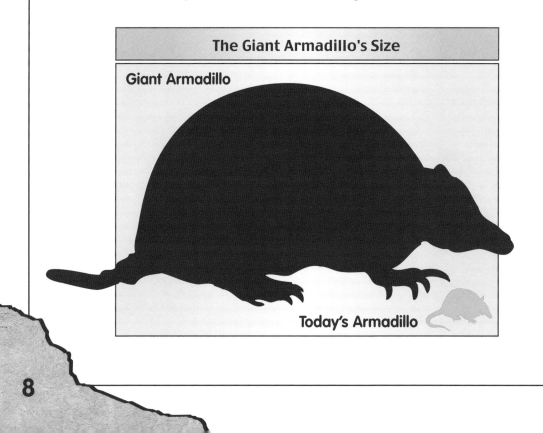

The Giant Armadillo's Size

Giant Armadillo

Today's Armadillo

The armadillo is the only mammal with a true shell. Like today's armadillos, the giant armadillo had a shell on its back. This shell was made of hard plates. These plates are called scutes. The giant armadillo also had plates on its head and tail.

This fossil is a piece of a giant armadillo's shell.

The prehistoric *Glyptodon* was a giant armadillo.

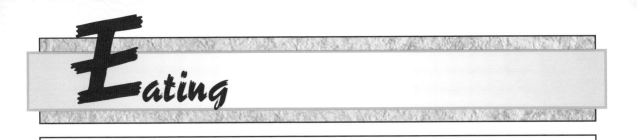

Today's armadillos eat ants, termites, and other insects. They eat fruits and small animals, too. The giant armadillo probably ate the same things. It may have used its long nose to smell for food. The giant armadillo probably dug up underground insects with its claws.

The giant armadillo used teeth at the back of its mouth for chewing. It did not have front teeth.

11

Defense

The giant armadillo lived among many predators. Its shell may have protected it from some animals. Like a turtle, the giant armadillo could hide its head and legs inside its shell.

Turtles can hide inside their shells.

The giant armadillo's shell could not save it from bigger predators. Borhyaenids and saber-toothed cats could probably bite through its shell. Borhyaenids were dog-like meat eaters. Saber-toothed cats had knife-sized teeth.

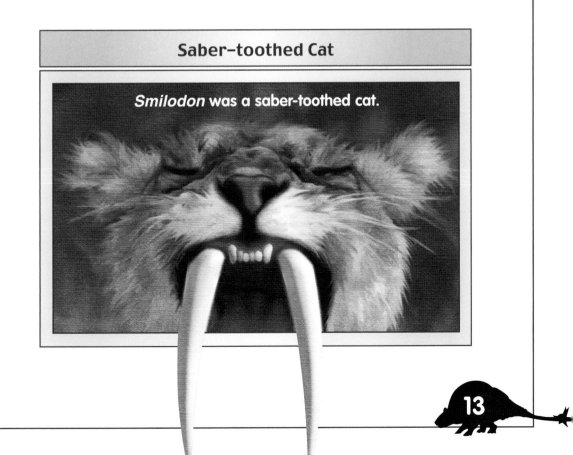

Saber–toothed Cat

Smilodon was a saber-toothed cat.

The Doedicurus

There were many kinds of prehistoric armadillos. One kind was called the *Doedicurus* (dee-dik-YOO-russ). On the end of the *Doedicurus's* tail was a bony club with spikes. Scientists believe it used its tail to fight other armadillos. Maybe the *Doedicurus* fought predators with its tail, too.

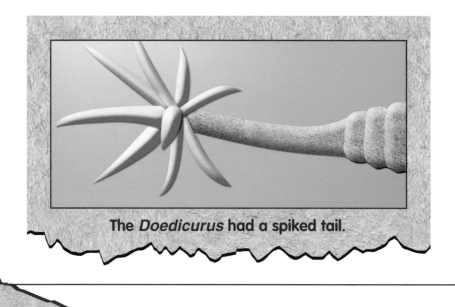

The *Doedicurus* had a spiked tail.

The *Doedicurus* looked a lot like the *Ankylosaurus*. The *Ankylosaurus* had hard plates all over its body. It had a club on the end of its tail, too. But the *Ankylosaurus* was a dinosaur. It was not related to the prehistoric armadillos.

This dinosaur looked like the *Doedicurus*.

Another Giant Armadillo

There is an armadillo around today that is commonly called "giant armadillo." Unlike other armadillos, it has as many as 100 small teeth. This giant armadillo has more teeth than any other land mammal.

Today's giant armadillo grows to become three feet (one m) long. It lives in South America and eats insects and snakes.

Scientists have names for important time periods in Earth's history. The giant armadillo lived during a time period called the Pleistocene. The Pleistocene began about two million years ago.

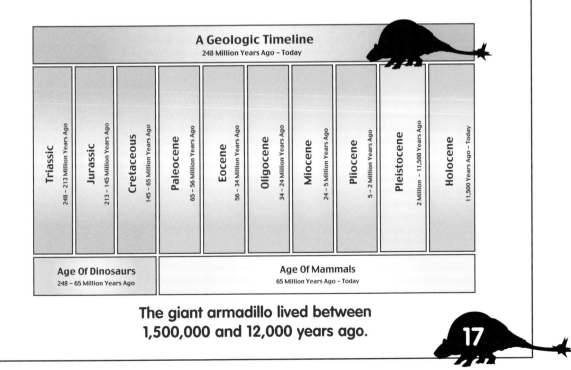

A Geologic Timeline
248 Million Years Ago – Today

Triassic	Jurassic	Cretaceous	Paleocene	Eocene	Oligocene	Miocene	Pliocene	Pleistocene	Holocene
248 – 213 Million Years Ago	213 – 145 Million Years Ago	145 – 65 Million Years Ago	65 – 56 Million Years Ago	56 – 34 Million Years Ago	34 – 24 Million Years Ago	24 – 5 Million Years Ago	5 – 2 Million Years Ago	2 Million – 11,500 Years Ago	11,500 Years Ago – Today

Age Of Dinosaurs	Age Of Mammals
248 – 65 Million Years Ago	65 Million Years Ago – Today

The giant armadillo lived between 1,500,000 and 12,000 years ago.

17

Giant armadillos lived in warm areas. Their fossils have been found in South America. They lived in southern parts of North America, too.

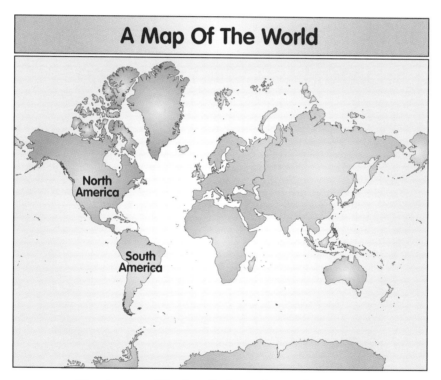

A Map Of The World

North America

South America

Giant armadillo fossils have been found in North America and South America.

Today, a land bridge joins North America and South America.

North America

Land Bridge

South America

At one time, North America and South America were not connected. Less than three million years ago, a land bridge formed between these two landmasses. Some animals, such as big meat eaters, crossed the land bridge to South America. Some of these meat eaters were deadly saber-toothed cats.

Giant armadillos died out about 12,000 years ago. Did saber-toothed cats kill all of them? Did they die from a great climate change or illness? Today's scientists are not sure why the *Glyptodon* died out. They hope to find the answer one day.

Saber–toothed Cat

The scimitar cat was a saber-toothed cat.

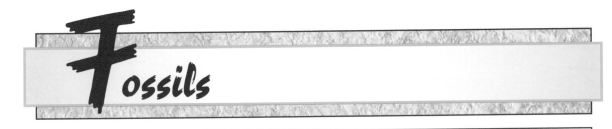

Fossils are important. They help people understand prehistoric animals and plants. A fossil can be a bone or a footprint. Remains of plants are fossils, too.

These children are looking at a fossil from the giant armadillo.

21

Richard Owen studied fossils in the 1800s. He was a famous scientist. Owen studied fossils from an animal no one knew about. He believed the animal was a prehistoric armadillo. In 1839, Owen named this prehistoric armadillo. He called it *Glyptodon*.

Richard Owen

Important Words

climate the weather of a place over time.

fossil remains of very old animals and plants commonly found in the ground. A fossil can be a bone, a footprint, or any trace of life.

mammal most living things that belong to this special group have hair, give birth to live babies, and make milk to feed their babies.

predator an animal that hunts and eats other animals.

prehistoric describes anything that was around more than 5,500 years ago.

scutes bony plates that make up a shell.

Web Sites

To learn more about the giant armadillo, visit ABDO Publishing Company on the World Wide Web. Web sites about the giant armadillo are featured on our Book Links page. These links are routinely monitored and updated to provide the most current information available.

www.abdopub.com

23

Index